D1201505

Horses

Appaloosa Horses

by Kim O'Brien

Consulting Editor: Gail Saunders-Smith, PhD

Capstone
press®

Mankato, Minnesota

Pebble Books are published by Capstone Press,
151 Good Counsel Drive, P.O. Box 669, Mankato, Minnesota 56002.
www.capstonepress.com

Books published by Capstone Press are manufactured with paper
containing at least 10 percent post-consumer waste.

Library of Congress Cataloging-in-Publication Data
O'Brien, Kim, 1960–
    Appaloosa horses / by Kim O'Brien.
    p. cm. — (Pebble books. Horses.)
    Includes bibliographical references and index.
    Summary: "A brief introduction to the characteristics, life cycle, and uses of the
Appaloosa horse" — Provided by publisher.
    ISBN-13: 978-1-4296-3303-1 (library binding)
    1. Appaloosa horse — Juvenile literature. I. Title. II. Series.
SF293.A7O27 2010
636.1'3 — dc22   2008048884

Note to Parents and Teachers

The Horses set supports national science standards related to
life science. This book describes and illustrates the Appaloosa
horse. The images support early readers in understanding the
text. The repetition of words and phrases helps early readers
learn new words. This book also introduces early readers to
subject-specific vocabulary words, which are defined in the
Glossary section. Early readers may need assistance to read
some words and to use the Table of Contents, Glossary, Read
More, Internet Sites, and Index sections of the book.

Table of Contents

Spotted Coats

Appaloosas are famous for their spotted coats. Appaloosas have many coat patterns.

Leopard Appaloosas have smaller spots all over. Blanket Appaloosas have spots on their hips.

Appaloosas have
thin manes and short tails.
They have muscular bodies.

Appaloosas have white rings around their eyes.
The skin around their mouths is freckled.

12

From Foal to Adult

Appaloosa foals
have coats
that change color
as they grow.

Appaloosas are adults after four years.
They stand 14.2 to 15.2 hands tall.

Horses are measured in hands.
Each hand is 4 inches (10 centimeters).
A horse is measured from the ground to its withers.

Riding Appaloosas

Appaloosas are fast
and sturdy.
Ranchers use Appaloosas
to herd cattle.

Appaloosas are calm.
They are fun to ride
on trails.

Appaloosas are smart
and gentle horses.
They work hard to please
their owners.

Glossary

coat — the hair covering a horse's body

foal — a young horse

freckles — the small dark spots on an Appaloosa's skin

gentle — kind and not rough

herd — to round up animals, such as cattle, and keep them together

mane — the hair that grows on the head and neck of some animals, such as horses and ponies

muscular — having strong muscles

pattern — a repeating set of colors or shapes

sturdy — strong and firm

Read More

Criscione, Rachel Damon. *The Appaloosa.* The Library of Horses. New York: Rosen, 2007.

Stone, Lynn M. *Appaloosa Horses.* Eye to Eye with Horses. Vero Beach, Fla.: Rourke, 2008.

Internet Sites

FactHound offers a safe, fun way to find Internet sites related to this book. All of the sites on FactHound have been researched by our staff.

Here's all you do:

Visit *www.facthound.com*

FactHound will fetch the best sites for you!

Index

Word Count: 108
Grade: 1
Early-Intervention Level: 18

Editorial Credits
Sarah L. Schuette, editor; Bobbi J. Wyss, designer; Jo Miller, media researcher

Photo Credits
Capstone Press/Karon Dubke, cover, 1, 4, 6, 8, 10, 12, 14, 18, 20
Kimball Stock/Ron Kimball, 16

The author dedicates this book in memory of her grandmother, Katherine Boulware Sutton.